ractice in the Basic Skills **English 3**

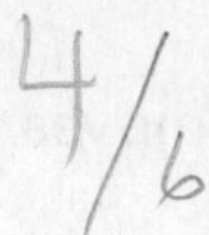

Contents

ished by Collins Educational
nprint of HarperCollins*Publishers* Ltd
5 Fulham Palace Road
lon W6 8JB

www.**Collins**Education.com
n-line support for schools and colleges

published 1978
edition published 2003
inted 10 9 8 7 6 5

ISBN-13 9780007177165

The authors assert the moral right to be identified as the authors of this work.

British Library Cataloguing in Publication Data
A catalogue record for this book is available from the British Library.

Illustrated by A Rodger

Printed by Gopsons Papers Ltd.,India

Verbs (1)

A Write down a word which shows how each of the following moves.

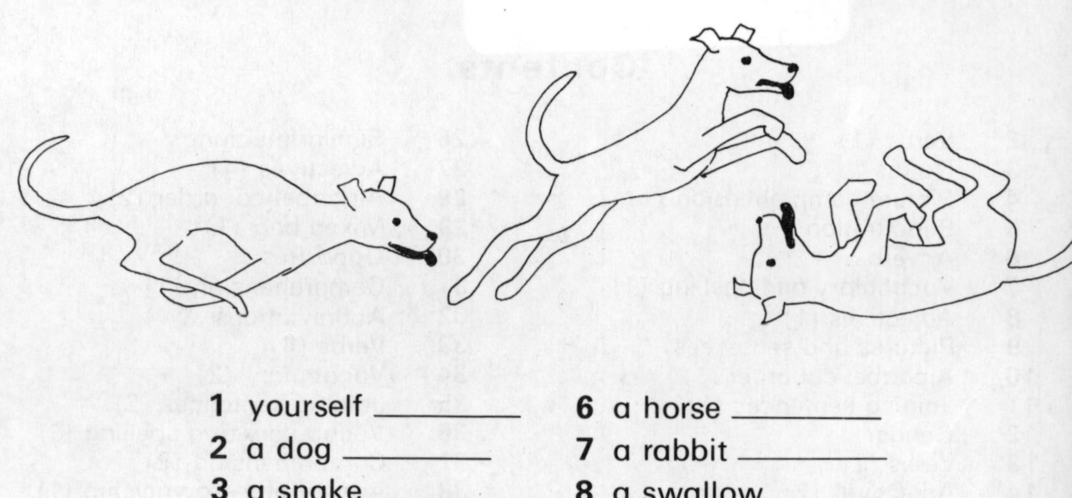

1 yourself ________
2 a dog ________
3 a snake ________
4 a cat ________
5 a frog ________
6 a horse ________
7 a rabbit ________
8 a swallow ________
9 a salmon ________
10 a monkey ________

B Write down a word which shows how each of the following moves.

1 a car ________
2 leaves ________
3 a ball ________
4 grass ________
5 an aeroplane ________
6 water ________
7 an elephant ________
8 a kite ________
9 snow ________
10 a clown ________

ouns

Write out the **nouns** in each of these sentences.

1 The horse was old.
2 I like chocolate.
3 The water is cold.
4 This apple is sour.
5 We ate our dinner.
6 The policeman caught the thief.
7 The cat climbed on the roof.
8 The boys and girls went to the cinema.
9 Leaves fell from the tree.
10 There are many books in the library.

Write down three things you might see

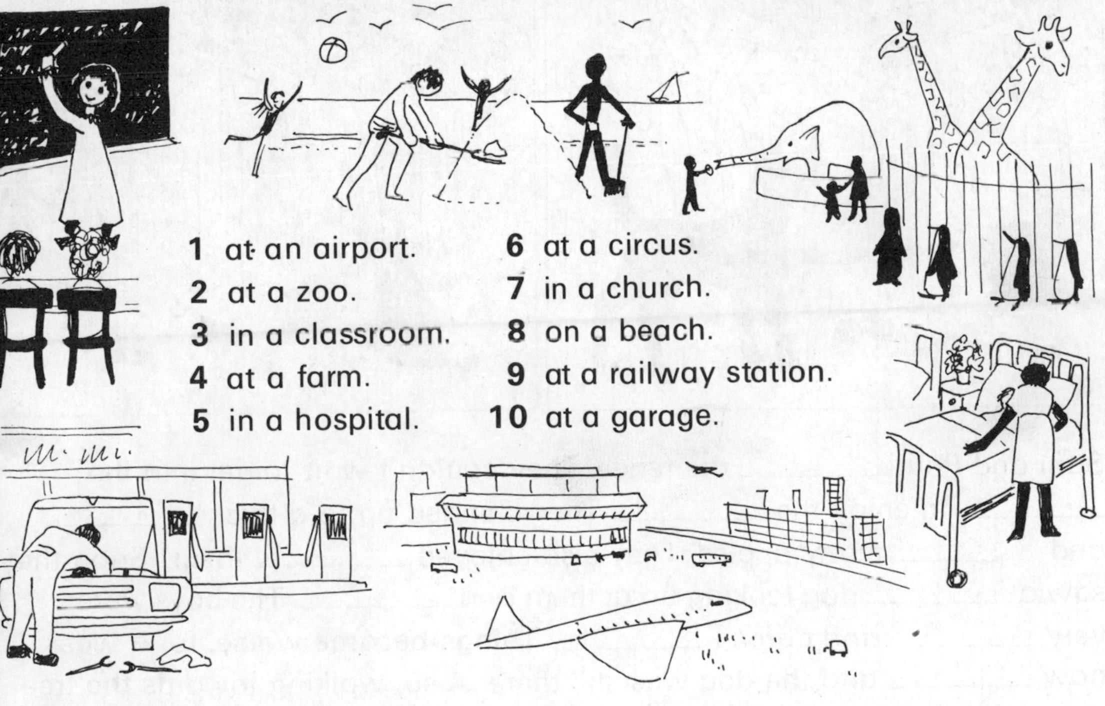

1 at an airport.
2 at a zoo.
3 in a classroom.
4 at a farm.
5 in a hospital.
6 at a circus.
7 in a church.
8 on a beach.
9 at a railway station.
10 at a garage.

Write the names of

1 five flowers. 2 five birds. 3 five trees.

Picture comprehension (1)

Write out the story filling in the twelve spaces by choosing your own words.

Sam and Paul _________ the fence. They couldn't wait to get into the _________ to enjoy the _________. They climbed up to a thick _________ and _________ many apples. They also enjoyed _________ them! Soon they saw a _________ dog looking up at them and _________. The boys were very _________ and daren't _________. Things became worse, for it was now _________ and the dog was still there. Also, walking towards the tree was the _________

Now write what you think happened next.

unctuation

Write a sentence about each picture.
Remember **capital letters** and **full stops.**

Write out these sentences putting in a **full stop** or a **question mark** at the end of each.

The Jumbo jet landed safely
Have you seen our new caretaker
A tortoise has a hard shell
We enjoyed Tim's party
Will you play football with me
Did you see that unusual bird
Our lawn needs cutting
Why don't you eat your dinner

Write out these sentences, putting in the missing **commas**.

The butcher sells lamb beef pork and sausages.
The cricket season is May June July August and September.
The sailor had been to China Japan India and Australia.
I saw snowdrops crocuses daffodils and tulips in the park.
Oak ash beech sycamore and elm are deciduous trees.
My favourite football teams are Everton Arsenal Motherwell Newcastle and Linfield.

Adverbs

A Complete each sentence by putting in the right **adverb** from the list below.

1 Snow fell _________ on the mountain.

2 The girls ran _________ down the hill.

3 Anne slept _________ after her long swim.

4 Our team won the swimming gala _________ this year.

5 The sun shone _________ all morning.

6 The old man walked _________ up the stairs.

7 Bill bought his bicycle _________ at the sale.

8 The hungry dog ate his food _________.

brightly	greedily	quickly	cheaply
heavily	easily	slowly	soundly

B Add an **adverb** to complete each sentence.

1 Derek tied the rope _________.

2 Alan behaved very _________.

3 Grandma could not cross the road _________.

4 The nurse treated her patient _________.

5 When our team scored we all cheered _________.

6 I can do those sums _________.

7 Tom painted his picture _________.

8 The crane lifted the steel bars _________.

ocabulary and spelling (1)

The answers to these clues all end in **ey**.

Used to open a lock. __ __ __
Bees make this sweet food. __ __ __ __ __
Like a small horse with big ears. __ __ __ __ __ __
Bank notes and coins. __ __ __ __ __
Smoke goes up one. __ __ __ __ __ __ __
A small animal that lives in hot lands. __ __ __ __ __ __

The answers to these clues all end in **aw**.

A metal blade with teeth for cutting. __ __ __
An animal's foot with claws. __ __ __
Dry stalks of cut corn. __ __ __ __ __
Everyone must obey the __ __ __.
The lower part of your face. __ __ __
To make a picture of something. __ __ __ __

The answers to these clues all end in **le**.

A two-wheeled vehicle. __ __ __ __ __ __ __
A fruit. __ __ __ __ __
A bird of prey. __ __ __ __ __
A gun with a long barrel. __ __ __ __ __
Burned to give light. __ __ __ __ __ __
A referee uses one. __ __ __ __ __ __ __

Adjectives (1)

A Write out the **adjectives** in these sentences.

1 Jayne wore a pink frock at her party.
2 Our football team wear blue shirts.
3 A big lorry skidded in the snow.
4 Mark played with his electric train.
5 The rabbit hid in the long grass.
6 A tall policeman helped the old lady to cross the road.
7 The tall cupboard was full of old books.
8 "Don't walk on the wet floor!" shouted the grumpy caretaker.
9 The long, thin rope was tied round the fat man's legs.
10 The huge tanker was rolling in the rough sea.

B Fit each of the **adjectives** in column A with the **nouns** in column B.

	A	B
1	juicy	sweater
2	hot	flower
3	fast	hill
4	heavy	orange
5	red	lake
6	loud	dinner
7	woollen	clown
8	deep	load
9	funny	noise
10	steep	car

ictures and sentences

/rite a sentence about each picture.
here are some words to help you.

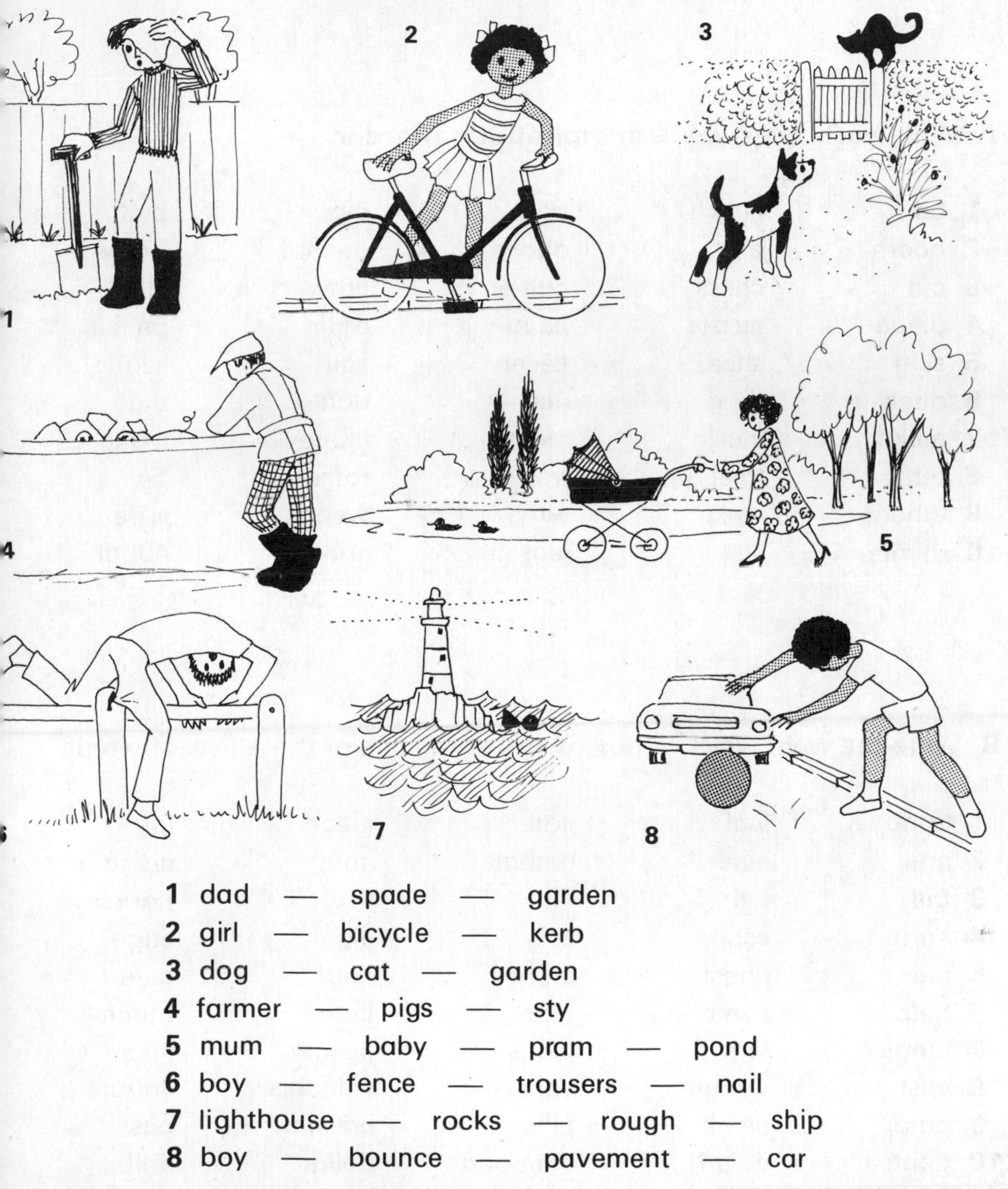

1 dad — spade — garden
2 girl — bicycle — kerb
3 dog — cat — garden
4 farmer — pigs — sty
5 mum — baby — pram — pond
6 boy — fence — trousers — nail
7 lighthouse — rocks — rough — ship
8 boy — bounce — pavement — car

Alphabetical order (1)

a b c d e f g h i j k l r

n o p q r s t u v w x y

A Write each list of words in **alphabetical order**.

1	bark	bench	bold	big	bull
2	acorn	air	above	animal	arrow
3	cut	chess	camel	crow	clock
4	place	puzzle	paint	pram	pencil
5	skin	shed	seven	sail	seal
6	duck	door	desk	dart	dig
7	milk	music	meat	money	make
8	tent	thief	talk	tomato	tie
9	wheat	wasp	wrist	week	wife
10	rhyme	rust	real	rain	ribbon

B Write the word which is **out of order** in each of these lists of words.

1	lamb	leaf	lion	lunch	log
2	nail	nine	netball	note	nurse
3	fall	fell	fill	fox	floor
4	earth	echo	eel	eight	edge
5	germ	ghost	giant	gold	glue
6	help	hymn	hide	hole	hutch
7	jungle	jam	jeans	jigsaw	joke
8	vest	village	valley	volcano	vulture
9	paint	pearl	pillar	present	past
10	dentist	dwarf	diamond	dollar	drill

oining sentences (1)

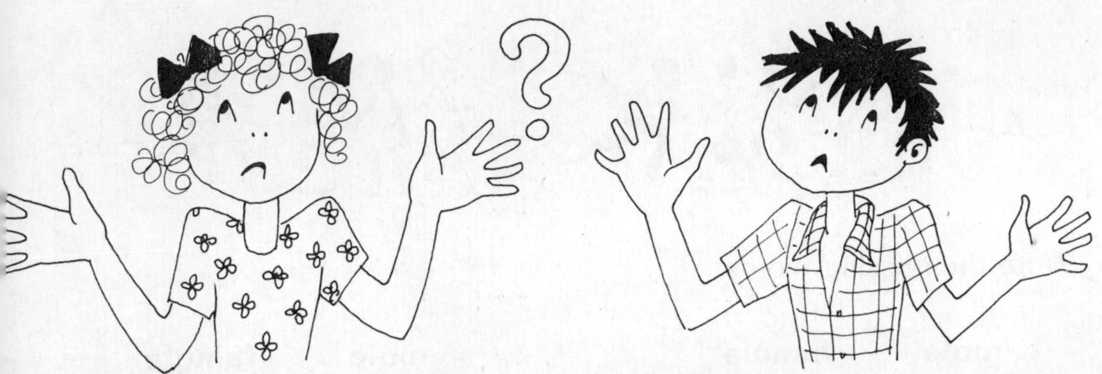

A Use **who** or **which** to join these sentences.
Remember: **who** for **persons**
which for **things**.

1 Here is the girl. She is a good swimmer.
2 I caught the dog. It bit the boy.
3 The teacher praised Tom. He had written an exciting story.
4 I thanked the policeman. He found my bike.
5 We travelled on the train. It went to Cardiff.
6 Jim caught a fish. It was swimming in the pond.
7 This is my aunty. She lives in Belfast.
8 Mrs. Rigby has two sons. They are very tall.

B Choose **so** or **but** or **because** to join each pair of sentences.

1 Tim slipped and fell. He did not hurt himself.
2 She had measles. She could not go to school.
3 Brenda returned the shoes to the shop. They were too small.
4 The hotel was burned down. No lives were lost.
5 She could not speak. She had a sore throat.
6 The garage was closed. We could not buy any petrol.
7 We went to the forest. We wanted to see a woodpecker.
8 The policeman chased the dog. He did not catch it.

Gender

A Write the missing words.

	male	female		male	female
1	prince	________	6	bridegroom	________
2	man	________	7	father	________
3	boy	________	8	wizard	________
4	uncle	________	9	grandfather	________
5	son	________	10	god	________

B Write the missing words.

	male	female		male	female
1	________	actress	6	________	waitress
2	________	mayoress	7	________	widow
3	________	queen	8	________	she
4	________	niece	9	________	heroine
5	________	sister	10	________	wife

C Write the missing words.

	male	female		male	female
1	________	lioness	6	________	cow
2	gander	________	7	fox	________
3	________	doe	8	________	ewe
4	stallion	________	9	cock	________
5	________	tigress	10	________	hind

erbs (2)

Find the **verbs** in these sentences.

1 The boy kicked the ball.
2 Janet ran down the street.
3 Tim jumped over the fence.
4 The car skidded on the ice.
5 The baby crawled on the rug.
6 Paul ate his tea and then played cricket.
7 The farmer cut the hedges and fed the cows.
8 The queen waved when we cheered her.
9 Sam cut his leg when he fell off the wall.
10 Our cat purrs when I stroke him.

Write down **two** actions which each of these persons might do.

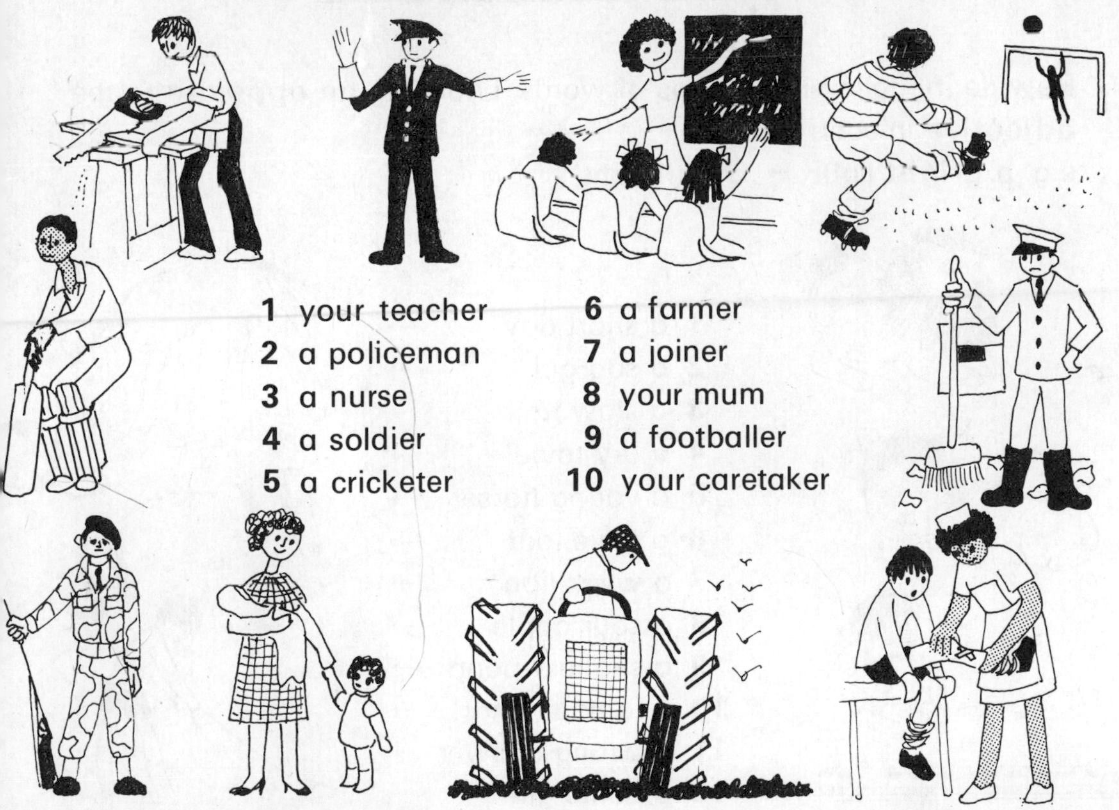

1 your teacher
2 a policeman
3 a nurse
4 a soldier
5 a cricketer
6 a farmer
7 a joiner
8 your mum
9 a footballer
10 your caretaker

Adjectives (2)

A Complete the following sentences by using the most suitable **adjective** from the list.

1 The __________ lights of the car dazzled me.
2 The __________ girl fell over the stool.
3 It took Jayne a long time to do the __________ sums.
4 The __________ kitten chased the ball of wool.
5 A __________ cloud usually brings rain.
6 The car skidded on an __________ patch on the road.
7 Our chimney blew down in the __________ weather.
8 Jack was an __________ boy and did not do his homework.

difficult	windy	bright	idle
dark	clumsy	icy	playful

B Rewrite the following groups of words, choosing an **opposite** to the **adjective** in each group.
e.g. a **bright** light → a **dull** light

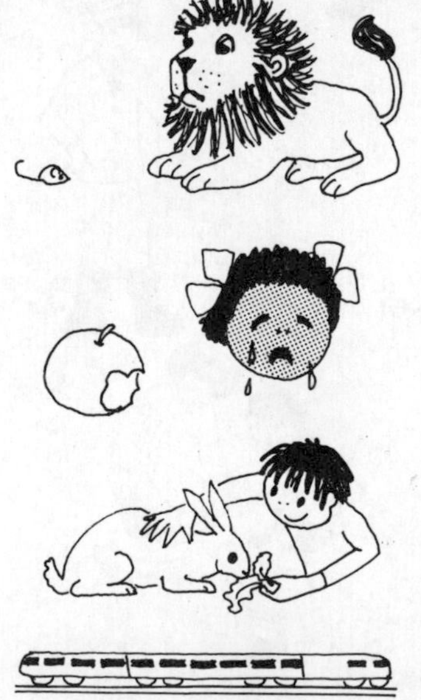

1 a short day →
2 a sad girl →
3 a slow train →
4 a dry towel →
5 a young horse →
6 a stale loaf →
7 a weak lion →
8 a sour apple →
9 a shallow pond →
10 a tame animal →
11 a wrong answer →
12 a polite girl →

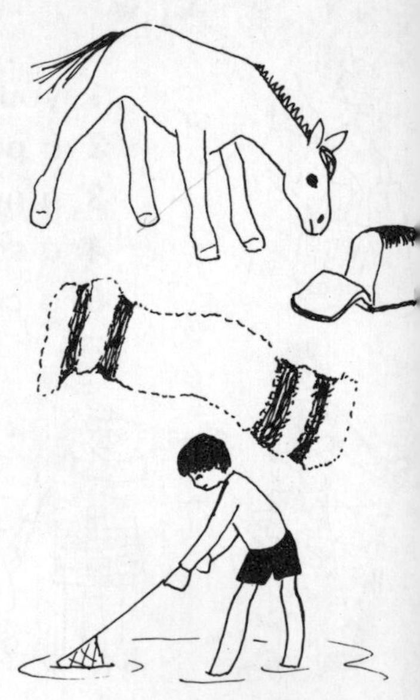

Plurals

Write the correct **plurals** of these words.

A

1 dog
2 box
3 brush
4 girl
5 hand
6 glass
7 match
8 lake
9 fox
10 flower

B

1 holiday
2 city
3 army
4 boy
5 key
6 story
7 monkey
8 pony
9 lady
10 valley

C

1 half
2 cargo
3 loaf
4 thief
5 potato
6 wolf
7 volcano
8 leaf
9 elf
10 tomato

D

1 day
2 scarf
3 chief
4 lily
5 child
6 church
7 piano
8 woman
9 foot
10 paper

Pronouns

Remember: a **pronoun** is a word used in place of a **noun**.

A Write out the **pronouns** in these sentences.

1 I am now nine years old.
2 He jumped over the fence.
3 She baked a large cake.
4 Please pass me a ruler.
5 They are going to the cinema.
6 You must eat all your dinner.
7 We enjoyed the party. Did you?
8 There is a dog called Kim. It is an Alsatian.

B Write out these sentences and put a **pronoun** in place of the **noun** or **nouns** in bold type.

1 **Janet** won the first race.
2 The **dog** ran off when I opened the door.
3 **Pat** and **Sue** are busy painting.
4 The **rain** is still pouring down.
5 Peter chose the **flowers** for his mother.
6 **Mr. Clark** dug his garden.
7 Brian gave stamps to **Mrs. Kay**.
8 Tom asked **Bill** for some sweets.

it	he	they	she	him	her	them

Adjectives (3)

A Use the vowels **a e i o u** to complete these **adjectives**.

very unkind	c r ___ ___ l
angry, wild	f ___ ___ r c ___
kind, showing friendship	f r ___ ___ n d l y
not costing much money	c h ___ ___ p
not making any sound	s ___ l ___ n t

B In each line write out the **adjective** which **best** describes the word in heavy type.

1 elephant	hungry	huge	tiny	quick
2 tree	square	purple	iron	leafy
3 fire	blazing	happy	damp	wet
4 chair	three-legged	playful	comfortable	sleepy
5 horse	smiling	bold	grassy	fast
6 water	wet	fresh	loud	woollen
7 street	busy	grassy	broken	speedy
8 gale	calm	small	howling	warm
9 orange	oblong	juicy	green	musical
10 book	babbling	lazy	wooden	exciting

C Complete each sentence by choosing a suitable **adjective**.

1 We were very happy when we heard the __________ news.
2 The fireman received a medal for his __________ act.
3 The old lady stumbled along carrying a __________ bag.
4 The boat overturned in the __________ sea.
5 Jean enjoyed eating the __________ pear.

Picture comprehension (2)

Look carefully at the four pictures. Write two sentences about each picture so that you tell the story. Give your story a title.
These words will help you.

man	dig	garden	kettle	bird	eggs
cat	fence	pounce	table	hatched	pleased

Vocabulary and spelling (2)

A The answers to these clues all have **tt** in them.

1 Opposite of top. __ __ t t __ __
2 Bad. __ __ t t __ __
3 A small room in the roof. __ t t __ __
4 A food made from milk __ __ t t __ __
5 A small country house. __ __ t t __ __ __
6 Nice to look at. __ __ __ t t __

B The answers to these clues all have **rr** in them.

1 A looking glass. __ __ r r __ __
2 Not wide. __ __ r r __ __
3 The day after today. __ __ __ __ r r __ __
4 To go quickly. __ __ r r __
5 A soft, juicy, red fruit. __ __ __ __ __ __ __ r r __
6 Used with a bow for shooting. __ r r __ __

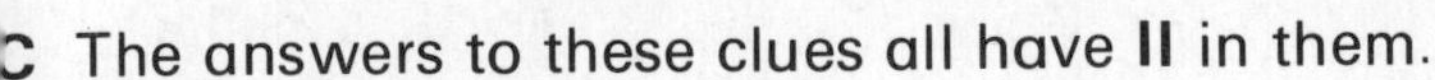

C The answers to these clues all have **ll** in them.

1 Dancing to music on a stage. __ __ l l __ __
2 A small bird with a forked tail. __ __ __ l l __ __
3 The colour of buttercup flowers. __ __ l l __ __
4 High. __ __ l l
5 A dog wears one round its neck. __ __ l l __ __
6 A number of houses in the country. __ __ l l __ __ __

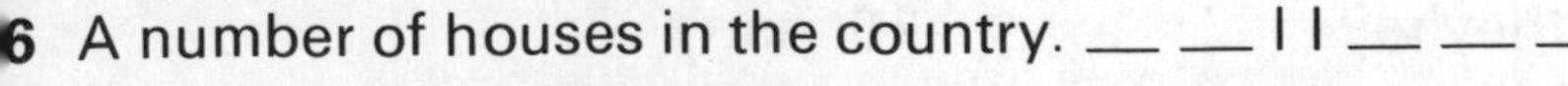

Contractions

A Join each pair of words together and write the short form.
Remember: the **apostrophe (')** goes where the **i** was.

1 he is
2 she is
3 it is
4 who is
5 that is
6 where is
7 what is
8 there is

B Join each pair of words together and write the short form.
Remember: the **apostrophe (')** goes where the **wi** was.

1 we will
2 he will
3 you will
4 she will
5 I will
6 they will

C Join each pair of words together and write the short form.

1 we are
2 I am
3 they are
4 we have
5 they have
6 I have

D Write these short forms in full.

1 doesn't
2 weren't
3 haven't
4 we'll
5 they're
6 I'm
7 that's
8 they'll
9 when's
10 can't

Groups

A Choose a group name from the list below to complete each line.

1 bear kangaroo tiger monkey →
2 blue red green yellow →
3 spanner saw plane hammer →
4 lemon peach strawberry orange →
5 van car lorry taxi →
6 June October May December →
7 sycamore willow beech oak →
8 shark cod plaice sardine →
9 daffodil pansy daisy snowdrop →
10 robin sparrow thrush duck →

months tools flowers colours trees
birds mammals fish vehicles fruit

B In each of the following lines one word **does not** belong to the same group as the others.
Write the odd word.

1 oak ash tulip beech sycamore
2 England Jamaica Canada Asia Egypt
3 peach strawberry apple carrot lemon
4 tulip daffodil buttercup pansy grass
5 lorry ship car van bus
6 carpet stool chair bench settee
7 horse hen donkey cow sheep
8 knee ankle elbow wrist face

Verbs (3)

Write out the following sentences by choosing the most suitable **verb** from the brackets.

1 Tim was (hurled/thrown) off his bike when it hit the kerb.

2 Susan (walked/limped) off the field after she twisted her ankle.

3 Peter (stepped/leaped) on to the path as the lorry skidded towards him.

4 When the thunderstorm started we (went/dashed) for shelter.

5 The dinghy's sail was (ripped/pulled) to shreds by the raging gale.

6 The express train (travelled/thundered) through the station.

7 The soldiers (walked/marched) smartly to the palace.

8 The racing cars (drove/roared) along the straight at 260 km/h.

9 The scared pony (lashed/kicked) out at the snapping dog.

10 The water (gushed/dripped) from the burst pipe.

11 The brave man (went/dived) into the sea to rescue the little girl.

12 The thief (snatched/took) the old lady's handbag.

Picture comprehension (3)

Look carefully at the four pictures. Write a few sentences about each picture so that you tell a story. Give your story a title.
These words will help you.

Mark	Darren	zoo	entrance	price	monkey
grab	hat	swinging	bars	elephant	keeper
loaves	trunk	sea lion	leaping	feeding	throwing

Vocabulary (1)

A Which person would you link with each pair of words?

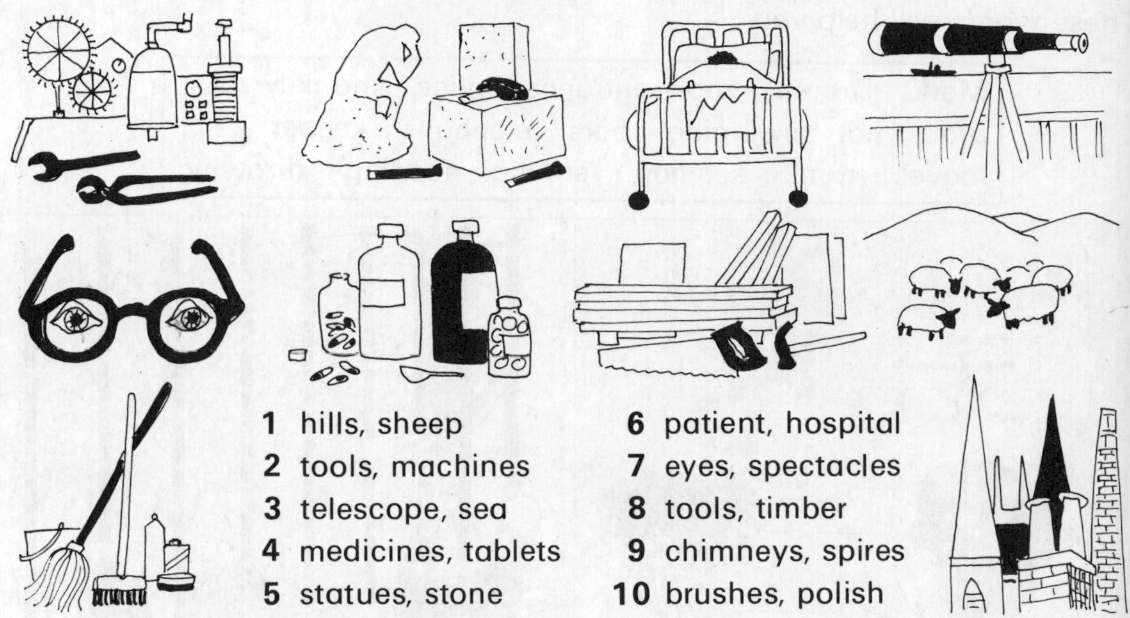

1 hills, sheep
2 tools, machines
3 telescope, sea
4 medicines, tablets
5 statues, stone
6 patient, hospital
7 eyes, spectacles
8 tools, timber
9 chimneys, spires
10 brushes, polish

chemist	caretaker	optician	joiner	mechanic
sculptor	shepherd	steeplejack	coastguard	nurse

B What name do you give to __________?
The first letter of each is given.

1 A woman who serves in a restaurant is a w__________.
2 Someone who draws and paints is an a__________.
3 The place where bread is made is a b__________.
4 Someone who looks after your teeth is a d__________.
5 The place where beer is made is a b__________.
6 Someone who searches for new lands is an e__________.
7 A person who repairs leaking water pipes is a p__________.
8 The place where many apple trees grow is an o__________.
9 Someone who rides horses in races is a j__________.
10 A land where very little grows is a d__________.

Questions

A Use the words from the list to complete the questions.
Don't forget the **question mark (?)** at the end of each question.

1 __ did you put the hamster's food
2 __ is your mother feeling after her operation
3 __ you enjoy your trip to the zoo
4 __ you lend me your bike, please
5 __ of these puppies would you like
6 __ were you not at school this morning
7 __ football boots are these
8 __ would you like to do tomorrow
9 __ you seen the exhibition of models
10 __ said that our team won

will	why	who	have	whose
did	where	which	what	how

B Here are Malcolm's answers to some questions.
Write down a question to fit each answer.

1 I live in Sutton, Surrey.
2 My favourite dog is a Dalmatian.
3 No, my sister isn't married.
4 My dad is a joiner.
5 I live on the fifth floor of Tower Flats.
6 Spurs is my favourite soccer team.
7 Yes, we went to Holland last year.
8 I hope to be an electrician.
9 My mum works in an office.
10 I enjoy soccer, reading and watching TV.

Similar meanings

A For each word in heavy type write a word which has a **similar** meaning. Choose from the list.

1 Paul found the maths **difficult**.
2 Dad took the **cash** to the bank.
3 Jayne was **weeping** because her dog was lost.
4 The joiner will **repair** the broken fence.
5 The **wealthy** singer drives a Rolls Royce.
6 Do you want me to **assist** you to push your car?
7 Carol was glad that her answers were **correct**.
8 Our school concert **commences** at 7.30 p.m.
9 Harvest mice are **small** animals.
10 The plumber is here to **connect** the water pipes.

rich	little	mend	right	hard
join	money	help	starts	crying

B Write out the word in each line which has a **similar** meaning to the word in heavy type.

1 **answer**	shout	reply	whisper	talk
2 **plucky**	strong	shy	brave	lucky
3 **bright**	show	flat	dull	shining
4 **fall**	drop	raise	run	swim
5 **reveal**	have	hide	show	receive
6 **collect**	sweep	gather	clean	jump
7 **short**	dark	tall	brief	long
8 **hide**	seek	ask	show	conceal
9 **sketch**	act	reveal	draw	dance
10 **top**	summit	base	middle	bottom

Adjectives (4)

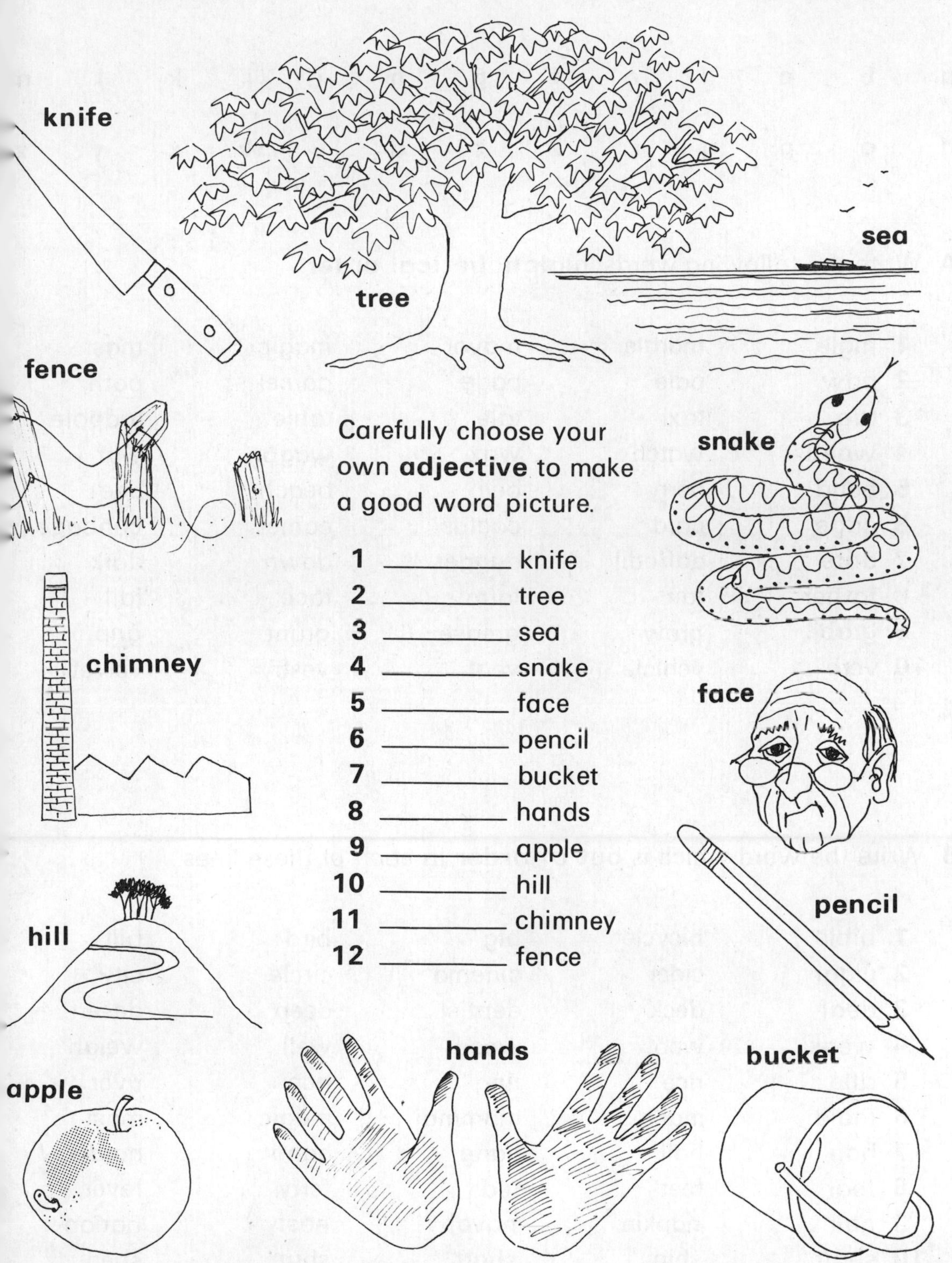

Carefully choose your own **adjective** to make a good word picture.

1 ____________ knife
2 ____________ tree
3 ____________ sea
4 ____________ snake
5 ____________ face
6 ____________ pencil
7 ____________ bucket
8 ____________ hands
9 ____________ apple
10 ____________ hill
11 ____________ chimney
12 ____________ fence

Alphabetical order (2)

a b c d e f g h i j k l m

n o p q r s t u v w x y z

A Write the following words in **alphabetical order**.

1	male	marble	mayor	magic	mast
2	paw	pale	page	parcel	path
3	tap	taxi	tale	table	tadpole
4	walrus	watch	wax	wagon	war
5	bend	berry	bell	beach	bee
6	cage	card	cactus	camel	cabbage
7	date	daffodil	dagger	dawn	dark
8	father	fair	farm	face	fall
9	grab	grow	grease	grunt	grip
10	verb	vehicle	veal	vestry	velvet

B Write the word which is **out of order** in each of these lines.

1	bible	bicycle	big	bird	bill
2	cigar	cider	cinema	circle	city
3	deaf	deck	dentist	deep	desert
4	weak	web	weed	well	weigh
5	rifle	rice	ring	ripe	river
6	maid	make	mammal	magic	mast
7	hair	hall	hang	hand	hard
8	fear	feet	fed	ferry	fever
9	nail	napkin	naval	nasty	nation
10	shaft	ship	short	shut	shed

[M]ixed bag (1)

Choose the correct word from the list to complete each sentence.

1 The football belongs to him. The football is ________.
2 The horses belong to them. The horses are ________.
3 The book belongs to you. The book is ________.
4 The apples belong to us. The apples are ________.
5 The bicycle belongs to me. The bicycle is ________.
6 The cat belongs to her. The cat is ________.
7 I bought a ball. The ball is ________.
8 Jayne has a new dress. The dress is ________.
9 They have some sweets. The sweets are ________.
10 You have a dog. The dog is ________.

mine	yours	his	ours	hers	theirs

[B] Complete these sentences by choosing suitable words from the list.

1 His face was as white as ________.
2 The miner's hands were as hard as ________.
3 Paul's hands were as black as ________.
4 Helen was as busy as a ________.
5 The stray dog was as thin as a ________.
6 Joan's hands were as cold as ________.
7 The bird's feathers were as green as ________.
8 This parcel is as heavy as ________.
9 My parcel is as light as a ________.
10 Her apple is as sweet as ________.

rake	honey	snow	bee	ice
nails	feather	coal	lead	grass

Opposites

A Write out the word with an **opposite** meaning to the word in capital letters in each line.

1	UNHAPPY	miserable	sad	glad	ill
2	GIVE	present	own	take	have
3	BEGIN	commence	run	end	start
4	GOOD	nice	neat	happy	bad
5	LARGE	small	thin	huge	tall
6	NOISE	shout	row	quiet	scream
7	CLEAN	bathed	dirty	washed	ill
8	HOT	cold	warm	sun	fire
9	DAY	afternoon	dawn	morning	night
10	SHALLOW	small	thin	deep	paddle

B Write out these pairs of words.
If they are **similar** in meaning write an S after them.
If they are **opposite**, write an O.

1 shout whisper
2 stay remain
3 found lost
4 first last
5 close near
6 ascend descend
7 separate unite
8 careful cautious
9 front back
10 clean pure
11 clean dirty
12 rich poor
13 fear terror
14 bleak dreary
15 hold release
16 colossal gigantic

omprehension (1)

Littlenose the bee keeper

During the Ice Age, boys like Littlenose ate many of the same ›ods as we do today. They had meat and fish as well as fruit and egetables, but they also ate things we would never dream of eating. ;aterpillars for instance. Littlenose knew nothing about sugar. He ever had sweets to eat, or jam, or sticky buns, or anything made from ugar. Instead he ate honey. Honey was found by taking it from the ests of wild bees. Collecting honey was as dangerous as hunting hinoceros or elk. The bees may have been small, but they were as erocious in their own small way as sabre-toothed tigers.

From *Littlenose to the Rescue* by John Grant
Reprinted by permission of BBC Publications

1 How do you know that Littlenose lived a long time ago?
2 Write down four foods he ate which we eat today.
3 What did he eat which you would not like to eat?
4 Write down the three things mentioned in the passage which we eat but Littlenose didn't eat.
5 Name two wild animals mentioned which we can still see today.
6 Name one wild animal from the passage which is extinct.
7 What was used instead of sugar?
8 From where did Littlenose get his honey?
9 Why was collecting honey dangerous?
10 How do you think the bees defended their nests?

Abbreviations

A Write the **abbreviation** for each of these words.
The list will help you.

1 Avenue
2 January
3 Road
4 September
5 Street
6 August
7 Terrace
8 December
9 Square
10 October

Sept.	Terr.
Ave.	Dec.
Sq.	St.
Aug.	Oct.
Jan.	Rd

B Write the **abbreviations** for each of the following.

1 Royal Air Force

2 On Her Majesty's Service

3 Doctor

4 Police Constable

5 Post Office

6 Her Majesty's Ship

7 United Kingdom

8 Victoria Cross

9 British Broadcasting Corporation

erbs (4)

hoose the correct **verb** to complete the sentences.

was or **were**

All the boys __________ playing football.
None of the animals __________ harmed by the fire.
They __________ making model planes.
Every girl __________ in the swimming pool.

is or **are**

Anybody __________ allowed to borrow a book.
Not one of the children __________ absent from school.
Every one of the bottles __________ broken.
All the children __________ visiting the museum.

C **ate** or **eaten**

1 Susan had __________ all her sweets.
2 The greedy dog __________ his food very quickly.
3 Many cabbage leaves had been __________ by caterpillars.
4 Jane __________ an apple on her way to school.

D **broke** or **broken**

1 A football __________ the classroom window.
2 This window has been __________ twice before.
3 Sue said that she had __________ the vase.
4 The vase __________ when Sue bumped into the table.

Vocabulary (2)

A Complete the following. The list of words will help you.

1 a ________ of pups
2 a ________ of sheep
3 a ________ of bees
4 a ________ of people
5 a ________ of cattle
6 a ________ of sailors
7 a ________ of teachers
8 a ________ of fish
9 a ________ of books
10 a ________ of trees
11 a ________ of flowers
12 a ________ of wolves
13 a ________ of soldiers
14 a ________ of ships

herd	crew	forest	litter	pack	fleet	swarm
bouquet	flock	regiment	library	crowd	staff	shoal

B Complete these sentences.

1 Bananas, mangoes and plums are all types of ________.
2 Freesias, lilies and carnations are all types of ________.
3 Salmon, tuna and herring are all types of ________.
4 Rubies, emeralds and sapphires are all types of ________.
5 Beetles, flies and grasshoppers are all types of ________.

C What would you expect to find

1 in a kettle ?
2 in an envelope ?
3 in a library ?
4 in a vase ?
5 in a gallery ?
6 in an aviary ?
7 in a greenhouse ?
8 in a hangar ?
9 in a safe ?
10 in a hutch ?
11 in a garage ?
12 in a sty ?
13 in a wardrobe ?
14 in a wallet ?
15 in a dustbin ?
16 in an aquarium ?

oining sentences (2)

hoose the best word from the list to join each of the two short sentences.

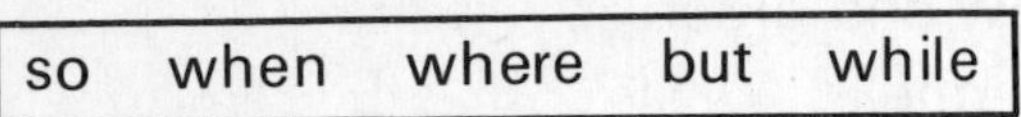

1 I went to the shed. I found a frightened puppy.
2 Mary was sleeping. We were playing.
3 It was muddy. We put on our wellingtons.
4 She did her best. She did not win the prize.
5 John was climbing a tree. He saw the fire.

B

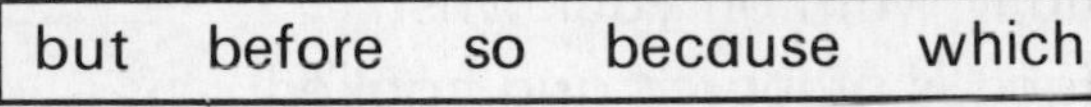

1 This is our secret cave. It is full of surprises.
2 David could not drink his tea. It was too hot.
3 Jenny looked for her kitten. She could not find it.
4 Sam began to shiver. He put on his coat.
5 Derek had a bath. He went to bed.

C

1 We saw the policeman. He saved a lady from drowning.
2 The wind was very cold. It was the month of June.
3 Andrew was very clever. He was lazy.
4 Sue could not climb the rope. She tried her best.
5 Mark made a fire. Andrew put up the tent.

Vocabulary and spelling (3)

A The answers to these clues all have **ce** in them.

1 He helps to keep law and order. ___ ___ ___ ___ c e ___ ___ ___
2 A teacup stands on one. ___ ___ ___ c e ___
3 A large lump of ice that floats in the sea. ___ c e ___ ___ ___ ___
4 Part of something. ___ ___ ___ c e
5 A house for a king or queen. ___ ___ ___ ___ c e
6 Two times, or double. ___ ___ ___ c e
7 Doing something many times. ___ ___ ___ ___ ___ ___ c e
8 A time when there is no war. ___ ___ ___ c e

B The answers to these clues all have **tch** in them.

1 A small clock, usually worn on your wrist. ___ ___ t c h
2 The room where food is prepared and cooked. ___ ___ t c h ___ ___
3 A home for a pet rabbit. ___ ___ t c h
4 A bag sometimes carried by schoolchildren. ___ ___ t c h ___ ___
5 A mark made with something sharp. ___ ___ ___ ___ t c h
6 Looking at. ___ ___ t c h ___ ___ ___
7 To sew with thread. ___ ___ ___ t c h
8 Used by lame people to help them walk. ___ ___ ___ t c h ___ ___

C The answers to these clues all have **ck** in them.

1 A machine for telling the time. ___ ___ ___ c k
2 A covering for the foot and leg. ___ ___ c k
3 To hit with the foot. ___ ___ c k
4 A summer game. ___ ___ ___ c k ___ ___
5 A young farm bird. ___ ___ ___ c k ___ ___
6 A short coat. ___ ___ c k ___ ___
7 Cups, saucers and plates. ___ ___ ___ c k ___ ___ ___
8 Worn on a chain round the neck. ___ ___ c k ___ ___ ___ ___

omprehension (2)

It was a Sunday afternoon at the beginning of September. Ben was ·ing on the double bed which almost filled their small room. He was ·ading a comic, his hands cupped to his head, his legs in the air. Now nd then he shifted his position, licked a finger to his lips, and turned he pages of the comic. Max was standing by the window gazing out nto the back garden. He was watching his mother, who was by the ow wire fence which divided the bungalows. She was talking to the eople next door. They were called Johns. Mr. Johns was almost ald, his hair was white, and his face was brown, even in winter time. le didn't go to work; he never did anything except weed the garden nd smoke his pipe.

From *The Haunted Mine* by Richard Potts
Reprinted by permission of Pan Books Ltd.

1 In which room was Ben and what was he doing?
2 Did Ben live in a house or a bungalow?
3 What was the name of the next door neighbours?
4 Who else do you think shared the double bed with Ben?
5 What was Ben's mother doing?
6 What divided the gardens of the two bungalows?
7 Write two things which show that Mr. Johns was old.
8 How did Mr. Johns spend most of his time?
9 Why do you think his face was always brown?
10 Was Ben lying on his front or back? Give a reason for your answer.

The apostrophe—to show ownership (1)

A Write out the following using the **apostrophe (')** to show there is **one owner**.

e.g. David's book

1 the babys toy
2 Peters bike
3 the firemans helmet
4 the dogs kennel
5 the birds feathers
6 the deers antlers
7 the rabbits ears
8 the teachers table
9 the referees whistle
10 the horses tail
11 Carolyns car
12 the giraffes neck
13 the cars tyres
14 the lions claws
15 the gorillas cage
16 the policemans radio

B Write these the short way.

e.g. the spade which belongs to Sam → Sam's spade

1 the pen belonging to Mark →
2 the pram belonging to Jill →
3 the tent which belongs to Adam →
4 the heat of the sun →
5 the garage of the car →
6 the coat belonging to mum →
7 the cage of the parrot →
8 the petals of the flower →
9 the caravan belonging to Mr. Brown →
10 the tail of the cat →

ocabulary (3)

In each of the following groups, write out the one word which includes all the others.

1	girls	men	people	boys	women
2	Moscow	Paris	London	Brussels	capitals
3	apple	fruit	date	orange	pear
4	cabbage	lettuce	turnip	vegetables	cauliflower
5	supper	breakfast	dinner	tea	meals
6	football	cricket	tennis	games	squash
7	table	furniture	chair	cupboard	bookcase
8	drum	recorder	piano	organ	instruments
9	vehicles	van	bus	taxi	lorry
10	Glasgow	Belfast	cities	Swansea	Leeds

In each of the following groups, arrange the words in the order of size of the object, beginning with the smallest.

1	rat	pig	rabbit	horse	elephant
2	minute	week	second	day	hour
3	wren	starling	ostrich	seagull	turkey
4	city	village	house	country	continent
5	puddle	ocean	lake	sea	pond
6	cup	bath	kettle	eggcup	bucket
7	trunk	tree	twig	branch	leaf
8	shark	goldfish	cod	whale	shrimp
9	metre	millimetre	kilometre	centimetre	
10	yacht	liner	dinghy	rowing boat	supertanker

Verbs (5)

A Begin each of these sentences with **Yesterday**.
e.g. Anne **wins** the race.
Yesterday Anne **won** the race.

1 The dog **plays** in the garden.
2 The baker **bakes** a lot of bread.
3 The trawler **sails** to the White Sea.
4 Peter **arrives** at school at nine o'clock.
5 The farmer **chases** the dogs away from the sheep.
6 Paul **takes** a long time to do his maths.
7 Dad **drives** his car to the garage.
8 Tim **flies** his model aeroplane.
9 Sandra **feels** ill.
10 Our teacher **reads** a story to the class.

B Change the **verb** in bold type to show that something happens or is happening now.

1 The girl **spoke** with an American accent.
2 The boy **rubbed** his sore knee.
3 The thrush **hopped** about looking for worms.
4 Sarah always **found** time for reading.
5 Barry **brought** his young brother to school.
6 The dog **sat** outside the shop door.
7 The cars **stopped** at the traffic lights.
8 The workmen **dug** a deep hole.
9 The dog **begged** for a bone.
10 The bus **skidded** on the ice.

ocabulary and spelling (4)

The answers to these clues all have **pp** in them.

The last meal of the day. __ __ p p __ __
A fruit. __ p p __ __
Soft, comfortable shoes worn in the house. __ __ __ p p __ __ __
A reddish metal. __ __ p p __ __
A herring dried over smoke. __ __ p p __ __
A hot-tasting powdered spice. __ __ p p __ __
To come into sight. __ p p __ __ __
A small greyhound. __ __ __ p p __ __

The answers to these clues all have **gg** in them.

Cases and baggage used by a traveller. __ __ g g __ __ __
Turning over the soil. __ __ g g __ __ __
Someone who does throwing and balancing tricks. __ __ g g __ __ __
A short, sharp knife. __ __ g g __ __
The largest. __ __ g g __ __ __
To fight with something or someone. __ __ __ __ g g __ __
To laugh in a silly way. __ __ g g __ __
Rough and sharp at the edge. __ __ g g __ __

The answers to these clues all have **dd** in them.

To walk in shallow water. __ __ d d __ __
When people get married. __ __ d d __ __ __
The place where someone lives. __ d d __ __ __ __
The centre. __ __ d d __ __
A seat on a horse or a bicycle. __ __ d d __ __
A small, poisonous snake. __ d d __ __
Happening quickly. __ __ d d __ __ __ __
To interfere with something. __ __ d d __ __

Rhyming words

A Write out the word which **rhymes** with the word in bold type.

1 **pail**	fall	pill	sale	wall	fell
2 **pot**	goat	note	top	lit	knot
3 **die**	bee	high	say	may	lay
4 **done**	fun	sum	phone	wrong	gone
5 **pour**	our	low	for	fur	hour
6 **you**	bough	how	flew	bow	though
7 **frost**	post	lost	most	boast	toast
8 **bone**	none	sun	lone	won	bun
9 **care**	fear	here	fur	purr	hair
10 **knew**	bow	know	few	low	knot

B Write the missing word in each line. It must **rhyme** with the word in bold type.

1 **bawl**	A wren is a very ________ bird.
2 **floor**	Will you please ________ me a cup of tea?
3 **seat**	I shall ________ you outside the Post Office.
4 **bean**	Have you ________ my cat anywhere?
5 **flour**	The rose is my favourite ________.
6 **white**	I went to bed late last ________.
7 **fair**	It is rude to ________ at anyone.
8 **might**	I must ________ a letter to my pen friend.
9 **seek**	Pam was ________ after her long illness.
10 **date**	I had to ________ an hour for the bus.

he apostrophe—to show ownership (2)

Write out the following using the **apostrophe (')** to show that there is **more than one owner**.

1 the ladies hats
2 the dogs dinners
3 the policemens boots
4 the soldiers guns
5 the sheeps tails
6 the footballers shirts
7 the childrens books
8 the insects wings
9 the firemens hoses
10 the foxes cubs
11 the mices tails
12 the sailors ship
13 the womens shoes
14 the boys changing room
15 the miners lamps
16 the workmens hut

B Write these the short way.
e.g. the trunks of the elephants
the elephants' trunks

1 the club for boys
2 the cage of the wolves
3 the cloakrooms for pupils
4 a library for children
5 a staffroom for teachers
6 the dressing rooms of the footballers
7 the fangs belonging to the snakes
8 the meeting of the workers
9 a hairdresser for ladies
10 the babies of the mothers

Improving sentences

A In place of each **adjective** in heavy type choose another from the list which will improve the sentence.

1 The **hungry** dog was trapped for six days in a cave.
2 The Jumbo jet has **big** engines.
3 **Large** waves crashed over the ship caught on the rocks.
4 The pyramids are **old** buildings in Egypt.
5 The climber was trapped on the **dangerous** cliffs.
6 It is very **moist** in the jungle.
7 The fox is said to be a **sly** animal.
8 The tramp's **odd** behaviour puzzled us.

ancient	cunning	humid	powerful	enormous	strange	starving	perilous

B The man dived into the water to rescue the boy.

By using **adjectives** this sentence can be made more interesting.

The **brave** man dived into the **deep** water to rescue the **terrified** boy.

Improve these sentences by adding suitable **adjectives**.

1 Last winter we had _________ snow, _________ frosts and _________ gales
2 The _________ clowns wore _________ costumes at the circus.
3 Yesterday I saw a _________ man trying to cross a _________ road.
4 I enjoy a _________ _________ apple after my lunch.
5 The _________ motorist drove slowly in the _________ fog.
6 The _________ sheepdog rounded up the _________ sheep.
7 I saw the _________ firemen rescue two _________ ladies from the _________ house.
8 The _________ monkey climbed down the _________ tree and grabbed the _________ girl's ice cream.

ompound words

Write the name of each picture. Show the two words which form the **compound word**.

e.g. bull + dog → bulldog

Now use each word in a sentence.

Mixed bag (2)

A Complete the following with a suitable **noun**.

1 Uncle is to nephew as aunt is to ________.
2 Foal is to horse as lamb is to ________.
3 Hat is to head as shoe is to ________.
4 Honey is to bee as milk is to ________.
5 Sound is to ear as taste is to ________.
6 Ear is to hear as eye is to ________.
7 Sing is to bird as grunt is to ________.
8 Table is to wood as window is to ________.

B Which **verb** in the brackets means the **opposite** of the word in heavy type?

1 **move** (run gallop halt race walk)
2 **receive** (have buy give sell)
3 **arrive** (come depart stay enter)
4 **conceal** (hide reveal bury place)
5 **climb** (ascend scale soar rise descend)
6 **repair** (mend break make alter)
7 **shut** (fasten lock close open)
8 **defend** (protect attack help support)

C Complete each sentence with an **adverb** made from the word in bracket

1 The horse was galloping ________ towards the gate. (quick)
2 The nurses ________ lifted the injured boy. (careful)
3 The aeroplane landed ________ with a damaged engine. (safe)
4 Terry wrote his story very ________. (neat)
5 Grandad nodded his head ________. (sleepy)
6 The tortoise moved ________ across the grass. (slow)
7 The boys were working ________ on their canoe. (busy)
8 The lions roared ________ at their trainer. (angry)

milar sounding words

'rite out the sentences, completing them by choosing the correct word from e brackets.

1 My football cost £3 in the ________ at the sports shop. (sale, sail)
2 You must ________ your brother outside school. (meet, meat)
3 The bus ________ to town is now 12p. (fair, fare)
4 Sally was in ________ when she broke her arm. (pain, pane)
5 Mark looked ________ when he was ill in bed. (pale, pail)
6 Our house is on a busy ________ road. (mane, main)
7 A ________ tree hasn't any leaves. (bear, bare)
8 The football team lost ________ first match today. (their, there)
9 Please bring your book ________. (hear, here)
0 The car was too ________ so dad didn't buy it. (dear, deer)
1 We went on the dodgems at the ________. (fare, fair)
2 A lion has a long ________. (main, mane)
3 The ________ on the yacht was torn by the strong wind. (sale, sail)
4 The ________ is a timid animal. (dear, deer)
5 A ________ is a kind of bucket. (pale, pail)
6 John kicked the ball which broke a ________ of glass. (pain, pane)
7 I don't think the ________ is cooked enough. (meat, meet)
8 The polar ________ eats a lot of fish. (bare, bear)
9 Put the bicycle ________. (there, their)
0 Don't shout! I can ________ you. (hear, here)

Comprehension (3)

Cornerstones stood empty and deserted. The house had been like this for months. Even the 'For Sale' notice was looking old and neglected, slumped against the front gate-post where it had been blown by the wind. Behind the house, the large, rambling garden, from which you could look down into the town in one direction and across the hills in the other, was overgrown with weeds and grasses. In the orchard, last autumn's apples lay yellow and shrivelled beneath the bare trees in beds of damp leaves. *Cornerstones* itself had paint peeling from the front door, and the windows were shrouded with brown dirt.

From *Nobody's House* by Martin Hall

published by Fontana/Collins

1 What was *Cornerstones*?
2 Which two words show that no one lived at *Cornerstones*?
3 Did the house have a big or a small back garden?
4 What is an orchard?
5 Write down the two **adjectives** which describe the apples.
6 What was written on the notice board?
7 Was the house in a country district or in a town?
8 Write out the sentence which shows that the house needed repainting.
9 Was this description written in summer or winter? Give a reason for your answer.
10 Use a dictionary to find the meaning of:
deserted, neglected, slumped, shrivelled, shrouded.

nswers

age 2 Verbs (1)

1 – 10 Check your child's words.

1 – 10 Check your child's words.

age 3 Nouns

1 horse **2** chocolate **3** water **4** apple **5** dinner **6** policeman, thief **7** cat, roof
boys, girls, cinema **9** Leaves, tree **10** books, library

1 – 10 Check your child's answers.

Check your child's answers.

age 4 Picture comprehension (1)

heck your child's words are appropriate.

age 5 Punctuation

Check your child's use of capital letters and full stops.

1 The Jumbo jet landed safely.
Have you seen our new caretaker?
A tortoise has a hard shell.
We enjoyed Tim's party.
Will you play football with me?
Did you see that unusual bird?
7 Our lawn needs cutting.
8 Why don't you eat your dinner?
C 1 The butcher sells lamb, beef, pork and sausages.
2 The cricket season is May, June, July, August and September.
3 The sailor had been to China, Japan, India and Australia.
4 I saw snowdrops, crocuses, daffodils and tulips in the park.
5 Oak, ash, beech, sycamore and elm are deciduous trees.
6 My favourite football teams are Everton, Arsenal, Motherwell, Newcastle and Linfield.

Page 6 Adverbs

A 1 Snow fell **heavily** on the mountain.
2 The girls ran **quickly** down the hill.
3 Anne slept **soundly** after her long swim.
4 Our team won the swimming gala **easily** this year.
5 The sun shone **brightly** all morning.
6 The old man walked **slowly** up the stairs.
7 Bill bought his bicycle **cheaply** at the sale.
8 The hungry dog ate his food **greedily**.
B 1 – 8 Check that your child's adverbs are appropriate for the sentences.

Page 7 Vocabulary and spelling (1)

A 1 key **2** honey **3** donkey **4** money **5** chimney **6** monkey
B 1 saw **2** paw **3** straw **4** law **5** jaw **6** draw
C 1 bicycle **2** apple **3** eagle **4** rifle **5** candle **6** whistle

Page 8 Adjectives (1)

A 1 pink **2** blue **3** big **4** electric **5** long **6** tall, old **7** tall, old **8** wet, grumpy
9 long, thin, fat **10** huge, rough
B 1 juicy orange **2** hot dinner **3** fast car **4** heavy load **5** red flower **6** loud noise
7 woollen sweater **8** deep lake **9** funny clown **10** steep hill

Page 9 Pictures and sentences

1 – 8 Check that your child's sentences describe the pictures.

Page 10 Alphabetical order (1)

A 1 bark, bench, big, bold, bull
2 above, acorn, air, animal, arrow
3 camel, chess, clock, crow, cut
4 paint, pencil, place, pram, puzzle
5 sail, seal, seven, shed, skin
6 dart, desk, dig, door, duck
7 make, meat, milk, money, music
8 talk, tent, thief, tie, tomato
9 wasp, week, wheat, wife, wrist
10 rain, real, rhyme, ribbon, rust
B 1 lunch **2** nine **3** floor **4** edge **5** glue **6** hymn **7** jungle **8** valley **9** past **10** dwarf

Page 11 Joining sentences (1)

A 1 Here is the girl **who** is a good swimmer.
2 I caught the dog **who** bit the boy.
3 The teacher praised Tom **who** had written an exciting story.
4 I thanked the policeman **who** found my bike.
5 We travelled on the train **which** went to Cardiff.
6 Jim caught a fish **which** was swimming in the pond.
7 This is my aunty **who** lives in Belfast.
8 Mrs Rigby has two sons **who** are very tall.
B 1 Tim slipped and fell **but** he did not hurt himself.
2 She had measles **so** she could not go to school.
3 Brenda returned the shoes to the shop **because** they were too small.
4 The hotel was burned down **but** no lives were lost.
5 She could not speak **because** she had a sore throat.
6 The garage was closed **so** we could not buy any petrol.
7 We went to the forest **because** we wanted to see a woodpecker.
8 The policeman chased the dog **but** he did not catch it.

Page 12 Gender

A 1 princess **2** woman **3** girl **4** aunt **5** daughter **6** bride **7** mother **8** witch **9** grandmother **10** goddess
B 1 actor **2** mayor **3** king **4** nephew **5** brother **6** waiter **7** widower **8** he **9** hero **10** husband
C 1 lion **2** goose **3** buck **4** mare **5** tiger **6** bull **7** vixen **8** ram **9** hen **10** stag

Page 13 Verbs (2)

A 1 kicked **2** ran **3** jumped **4** skidded **5** crawled **6** ate, played **7** cut, fed **8** waved, cheered **9** cut, fell **10** purrs, stroke
B Check your child's answers.

Page 14 Adjectives (2)

A 1 bright **2** clumsy **3** difficult **4** playful **5** dark **6** icy **7** windy **8** idle
B 1 a long day **2** a happy girl **3** a fast train **4** a wet towel **5** an old horse **6** a fresh loaf **7** a strong lion **8** a sweet apple **9** a deep pond **10** a wild animal **11** a right/correct answer **12** a rude girl

age 15 Plurals

1 dogs **2** boxes **3** brushes **4** girls **5** hands **6** glasses **7** matches **8** lakes
foxes **10** flowers

1 holidays **2** cities **3** armies **4** boys **5** keys **6** stories **7** monkeys **8** ponies
ladies **10** valleys

1 halves **2** cargoes **3** loaves **4** thieves **5** potatoes **6** wolves **7** volcanoes
leaves **9** elves **10** tomatoes

1 days **2** scarves **3** chiefs **4** lilies **5** children **6** churches **7** pianos **8** women
feet **10** papers

age 16 Pronouns

1 I **2** He **3** She **4** me **5** They **6** You **7** We, you **8** It

1 She **2** It **3** They **4** It **5** them **6** He **7** her **8** him

age 17 Adjectives (3)

cruel, fierce, friendly, cheap, silent

1 huge **2** leafy **3** blazing **4** comfortable **5** fast **6** wet **7** busy **8** howling **9** juicy
exciting

1 Check your child's adjectives.

age 18 Picture comprehension (2)

heck your child's sentences explain what is happening in the pictures.

age 19 Vocabulary and spelling (2)

1 bottom **2** rotten **3** attic **4** butter **5** cottage **6** pretty

1 mirror **2** narrow **3** tomorrow **4** hurry **5** strawberry **6** arrow

1 ballet **2** swallow **3** yellow **4** tall **5** collar **6** village

age 20 Contractions

1 he's **2** she's **3** it's **4** who's **5** that's **6** where's **7** what's **8** there's

1 we'll **2** he'll **3** you'll **4** she'll **5** I'll **6** they'll

1 we're **2** I'm **3** they're **4** we've **5** they've **6** I've

1 does not **2** were not **3** have not **4** we will **5** they are **6** I am **7** that is **8** they
ill **9** when is **10** cannot

age 21 Groups

1 mammals **2** colours **3** tools **4** fruit **5** vehicles **6** months **7** trees **8** fish
flowers **10** birds

1 tulip **2** Asia **3** carrot **4** grass **5** ship **6** carpet **7** hen **8** face

age 22 Verbs (3)

thrown **2** limped **3** leaped **4** dashed **5** ripped **6** thundered **7** marched **8** roared
kicked **10** gushed **11** dived **12** snatched

age 23 Picture comprehension (3)

heck that your child's sentences explain what is happening in the pictures.

age 24 Vocabulary (1)

1 shepherd **2** mechanic **3** coastguard **4** chemist **5** sculptor **6** nurse **7** optician
joiner **9** steeplejack **10** caretaker

1 waitress **2** artist **3** bakery **4** dentist **5** brewery **6** explorer **7** plumber
orchard **9** jockey **10** desert

Page 25 Questions

A 1 Where did you put your hamster's food?
2 How is you mother feeling after her operation?
3 Did you enjoy your trip to the zoo?
4 Will you lend me your bike please?
5 Which of these puppies would you like?
6 Why were you not at school this morning?
7 Whose football boots are these?
8 What would you like to do tomorrow?
9 Have you seen the exhibition of models?
10 Who said that our team won?
B 1 - 10 Check that your child's questions are appropriate for the answers given.

Page 26 Similar meanings

A 1 hard **2** money **3** crying **4** mend **5** rich **6** help **7** right **8** starts **9** little **10** joi
B 1 reply **2** brave **3** shining **4** drop **5** show **6** gather **7** brief **8** conceal **9** draw **10** summit

Page 27 Adjectives (4)

1 – 12 Check that your child's adjectives are suitable.

Page 28 Alphabetical order (2)

1 magic, male, marble, mast, mayor
2 page, pale, parcel, path, paw
3 table, tadpole, tale, tap, taxi
4 wagon, walrus, war, watch, wax
5 beach, bee, bell, bend, berry
6 cabbage, cactus, cage, camel, card
7 daffodil, dagger, dark, date, dawn
8 face, fair, fall, farm, father
9 grab, grease, grip, grow, grunt
10 veal, vehicle, velvet, verb, vestry
B 1 bill **2** cider **3** deep **4** weigh **5** rice **6** magic **7** hand **8** fed **9** naval **10** shed

Page 29 Mixed bag (1)

A 1 his **2** theirs **3** yours **4** ours **5** mine **6** hers **7** mine **8** hers **9** theirs **10** yours
B 1 snow **2** nails **3** coal **4** bee **5** rake **6** ice **7** grass **8** lead **9** feather **10** honey

Page 30 Opposites

A 1 glad **2** take **3** end **4** bad **5** small **6** quiet **7** dirty **8** cold **9** night **10** deep
B 1 O **2** S **3** O **4** O **5** S **6** O **7** O **8** S **9** O **10** S **11** O **12** O **13** S **14** S **15** O **16** S

Page 31 Comprehension (1)

1 Littlenose lived a long time ago because he lived during the Ice Age.
2 Four foods that Littlenose ate which we eat today are meat, fish, fruit and vegetables.
3 Littlenose ate caterpillars which wouldn't be nice to eat.
4 Three things that Littlenose didn't eat but which we eat are sugar, jam and sticky buns.
5 Two wild animals which we can still see today are rhinoceros and elk.
6 An animal that is extinct is the sabre-toothed tiger.
7 Honey was used instead of sugar.

Littlenose got his honey from the nests of wild bees.
Collecting honey was dangerous because the bees were ferocious.
) Bees defend themselves by stinging people.

age 32 Abbreviations

1 Ave. **2** Jan. **3** Rd **4** Sept. **5** St. **6** Aug. **7** Terr. **8** Dec. **9** Sq. **10** Oct.
1 RAF **2** OHMS **3** Dr **4** PC **5** PO **6** HMS **7** UK **8** VC **9** BBC

age 33 Verbs (4)

1 were **2** was **3** were **4** was
1 is **2** is **3** is **4** are
1 eaten **2** ate **3** eaten **4** ate
1 broke **2** broken **3** broken **4** broke

'age 34 Vocabulary (2)

litter **2** flock **3** swarm **4** crowd **5** herd **6** crew **7** staff **8** shoal **9** library
0 forest **11** bouquet **12** pack **13** regiment **14** fleet
1 fruit **2** flowers **3** fish **4** jewels/gems **5** insects
1 water **2** letter **3** books **4** flowers **5** paintings **6** birds **7** plants **8** aeroplanes
money **10** a rabbit **11** a car **12** a pig **13** clothes **14** money **15** rubbish **16** fish

'age 35 Joining sentences (2)

1 I went to the shed **where** I found a frightened puppy.
Mary was sleeping **while** we were playing.
It was muddy **so** we put on our Wellingtons.
She did her best **but** she did not win the prize.
John was climbing a tree **when** he saw the fire.
1 This is our secret cave **which** is full of surprises.
David could not drink his tea **because** it was too hot.
Jenny looked for her kitten **but** she could not find it.
Sam began to shiver **so** he put on his coat.
Derek had a bath **before** he went to bed.
1 We saw the policeman **who** saved a lady from drowning.
The wind was very cold **yet** it was the month of June.
Andrew was very clever **but** he was lazy.
Sue could not climb the rope **though** she tried her best.
Mark made a fire **while** Andrew put up the tent.

age 36 Vocabulary and spelling (3)

A 1 policeman **2** saucer **3** iceberg **4** piece **5** palace **6** twice **7** practice **8** peace
B 1 watch **2** kitchen **3** hutch **4** satchel **5** scratch **6** watching **7** stitch **8** crutches
C 1 clock **2** sock **3** kick **4** cricket **5** chicken **6** jacket **7** crockery **8** necklace

Page 37 Comprehension (2)

1 Ben was in the bedroom reading a comic.
2 Ben lived in a bungalow.
3 The neighbours' name was the Johns.
4 Ben shared the double bed with Max.
5 Ben's mother was talking to the people next door.
6 The two gardens were divided by a low wire fence.
7 Two things which show that Mr. John was old are
his almost bald head and white hair.

8 Mr. Johns spent most of his time weeding the garden.
9 Mr. John's face was always brown because he was always outside in the garde
10 Ben was lying on his front because he was resting on his hands and had to shi his position to turn the pages of his comic.

Page 38 The apostrophe – to show ownership (1)

A 1 the baby's toy **2** Peter's bike **3** the fireman's helmet **4** the dog's kennel **5** the bird's feathers **6** the deer's antlers **7** the rabbit's ears **8** the teacher's table **9** the referee's whistle **10** the horse's tail **11** Carolyn's car **12** the giraffe's neck **13** the car's tyres **14** the lion's claws **15** the gorilla's cage **16** the policeman's radi
B 1 Mark's pen **2** Jill's pram **3** Adam's tent **4** the sun's heat **5** the car's garage **6** mum's coat **7** the parrot's cage **8** the flower's petals **9** Mr Brown's caravan **10** the cat's tail

Page 39 Vocabulary (3)

A 1 people **2** capitals **3** fruit **4** vegetables **5** meals **6** games **7** furniture **8** instruments **9** vehicles **10** cities
B 1 rat, rabbit, pig, horse, elephant
2 second, minute, hour, day, week
3 wren, starling, seagull, turkey, ostrich
4 house, village, city, country, continent
5 puddle, pond, lake, sea, ocean
6 eggcup, cup, kettle, bucket, bath
7 leaf, twig, branch, trunk, tree
8 shrimp, goldfish, cod, shark, whale
9 millimetre, centimetre, metre, kilometre
10 dinghy, rowing boat, yacht, liner, supertanker

Page 40 Verbs (5)

A 1 Yesterday the dog **played** in the garden.
2 Yesterday the baker **baked** a lot of bread.
3 Yesterday the trawler **sailed** to the White Sea.
4 Yesterday Peter **arrived** at school at nine o'clock.
5 Yesterday the farmer **chased** the dogs away from the sheep.
6 Yesterday Paul **took** a long time to do his maths.
7 Yesterday Dad **drove** his car to the garage.
8 Yesterday Tim **flew** his model aeroplane.
9 Yesterday Sandra **felt** ill.
10 Yesterday our teacher **read** a story to the class.
B 1 The girl **speaks/is speaking** with an American accent.
2 The boy **rubs/is rubbing** his sore knee.
3 The thrush **hops/is hopping** about looking for worms.
4 Sarah always **finds** time for reading.
5 Barry **brings/is bringing** his young brother to school.
6 The dog **sits/is sitting** outside the shop door.
7 The cars **stop/are stopping** at the traffic lights.
8 The workmen **dig/are digging** a deep hole.
9 The dog **begs/is begging** for a bone.
10 The bus **skids/is skidding** on the ice.

Page 41 Vocabulary and spelling (4)

A 1 supper 2 apple 3 slippers 4 copper 5 kipper 6 pepper 7 appear 8 whippet
B 1 luggage 2 digging 3 juggler 4 dagger 5 biggest 6 struggle 7 giggle
8 jagged
C 1 paddle 2 wedding 3 address 4 middle 5 saddle 6 adder 7 suddenly
8 meddle

Page 42 Rhyming words

A 1 sale 2 knot 3 high 4 fun 5 for 6 flew 7 lost 8 lone 9 hair 10 few
B 1 tall 2 pour 3 meet 4 seen 5 flower 6 night 7 stare 8 write 9 weak 10 wait

Page 43 The apostrophe – to show ownership (2)

A 1 the ladies' hats
2 the dogs' dinners
3 the policemen's boots
4 the soldiers' guns
5 the sheep's tails
6 the footballers' shirts
7 the children's books
8 the insects' wings
9 the firemen's hoses
10 the foxes' cubs
11 the mice's tails
12 the sailors' ship
13 the women's shoes
14 the boys' changing room
15 the miners' lamps
16 the workmen's hut
B 1 the boys' club
2 the wolves' cage
3 the pupils' cloakroom
4 the children's library
5 the teachers' staffroom
6 the footballers' dressingrooms
7 the snake's fangs
8 the workers' meeting
9 the ladies' hairdresser
10 the mothers' babies

Page 44 Improving sentences

A 1 The **starving** dog was trapped for six days in a cave.
2 The Jumbo has **powerful** engines.
3 **Enormous** waves crashed over the ship caught on the rocks.
4 The pyramids are **ancient** buildings in Egypt.
5 The climber was trapped on the **perilous** cliffs.
6 It is very **humid** in the jungle.
7 The fox is said to be a **cunning** animal.
8 The tramp's **strange** behaviour puzzled us.
B Check your child has used suitable adjectives to complete the sentences.

Page 45 Compound words
A 2 wheel + barrow = wheelbarrow
3 water + fall = waterfall
4 butter + fly = butterfly
5 wind + mill = windmill
6 trap + door = trapdoor
7 port + hole = porthole
8 arm + chair = armchair
9 tooth + brush = toothbrush
10 black + board = blackboard
11 light + house = lighthouse
12 cup + board = cupboard
B Check your child's sentences.

Page 46 Mixed bag (2)
A 1 niece **2** sheep **3** foot **4** cow **5** tongue **6** see **7** pig **8** glass
B 1 halt **2** give **3** depart **4** reveal **5** descend **6** break **7** open **8** attack
C 1 quickly **2** carefully **3** safely **4** neatly **5** sleepily **6** slowly **7** busily **8** angrily

Page 47 Similar sounding words
1 sale **2** meet **3** fare **4** pain **5** pale **6** main **7** bare **8** their **9** here **10** dear **11** fair
12 mane **13** sail **14** deer **15** pail **16** pane **17** meat **18** bear **19** there **20** hear

Page 48 Comprehension (3)
1 *Cornerstones* was a house.
2 Two words that show that no one lived at *Cornerstones* are 'empty' and 'deserted'.
3 It had a big back garden.
4 An orchard is where fruit trees grow.
5 Two adjectives that describe the apples are 'yellow' and 'shrivelled'.
6 'For Sale' was written on the notice board.
7 The house was in a country district.
8 The sentence which shows that the house needed repainting is: '*Cornerstones* itself had paint peeling from the front door...'
9 The description was written in winter because it states: 'last autumn's apples...'.
10 deserted – empty
neglected – not been cared for
slumped – fallen heavily or suddenly
shrivelled – to be shrunken and withered
shrouded – covered